Photocopiable Art for the Liturgical Year
Seasons to Celebrate

Cecilia Duval RJM

First published in 1998 in Great Britain by
KEVIN MAYHEW LTD
Rattlesden
Bury St Edmunds
Suffolk IP30 0SZ

ISBN 1 84003 190 5
Catalogue No 1396062

0 1 2 3 4 5 6 7 8 9

Cover illustration by Cecilia Duval
Cover design by Jaquetta Sergeant
Printed in Great Britain

Introduction

This book is intended to be used as a resource in which attention is focused on the inner meaning of particular liturgical themes encountered throughout the year.

The images expressed in black and white attempt to establish contact with the spiritual message inherent in the rites, readings and prayers of the different liturgical seasons.

In many instances the inspiration has been found in the architecture, sculpture and mosaics of the early and medieval Church. Where possible, the source of my ideas is indicated. Otherwise, the interpretation is personal.

Some of the examples may be of use in planning banner and poster designs, but it is advisable to remember the difference in scale, as well as the choice of colour, materials and siting of the finished work.

The logo of the Burning Bush is interpreted as a symbol of the awe and reverence of Moses in approaching Yahweh hidden in the bush, which 'was burning but not consumed'.

CECILIA DUVAL RJM

Contents

Advent

1   There will be signs in the sun and moon and stars.
Luke 1:25

2   The people that walked in darkness have seen a great light.
Isaiah 9:1

3   Repent for the kingdom of heaven is close at hand.
Matthew 3:2

4   Prepare a way for the Lord,
make his paths straight.
Luke 3:4

1

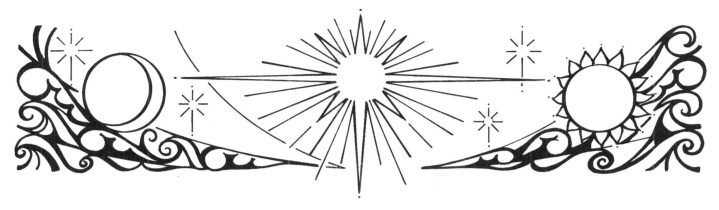

2

3

4

The Great 'O' Antiphons

The Great 'O' Antiphons are seven ancient prayers using Old Testament titles of the Messiah. They precede and follow the Magnificat during the last week of Advent, and express our longing for God.

1   O Wisdom, you come forth from the mouth of the Most High.
    You fill the universe and hold all things together
    in a strong yet gentle manner.
    O come to teach us the way of truth.

Wisdom

2 O Adonai and leader of Israel,
   you appeared to Moses in a burning bush
   and you gave him the Law on Sinai.
   O come and save us with your mighty power.

Adonai

3 O Shoot of Jesse, you stand as a signal for the nations;
   kings fall silent before you whom the peoples acclaim.
   O come to deliver us, and do not delay.

Shoot of Jesse

4　O Key of David and sceptre of Israel,
　　what you open no one else can close again;
　　what you close no one can open.
　　O come to lead the captive from prison;
　　free those who sit in darkness and in the shadow of death.

Key of David

5   O Dayspring, you are the splendour of eternal light
    and the sun of justice.
    O come and enlighten those who sit in darkness
    and in the shadow of death.

Dayspring

6 O King whom all the peoples desire,
   you are the cornerstone which makes all one.
   O come and save man whom you made from clay.

King

7 O Emmanuel, you are our king and judge,
the One whom the peoples await and their Saviour.
O come and save us, Lord, our God.

Emmanuel

Christmas 1

The angel of the Lord appeared to them.
Luke 2:9

TODAY A SAVIOUR HAS BEEN BORN TO YOU; HE IS CHRIST THE LORD.

Christmas 2

A little child is born for us,
and he shall be called the mighty God.

Epiphany

1 'We saw his star as it rose
   and we have come to do him homage.'
   Matthew 2:2

2 Opening their treasures,
   they offered him gifts of gold,
   frankincense and myrrh.
   Matthew 2:11

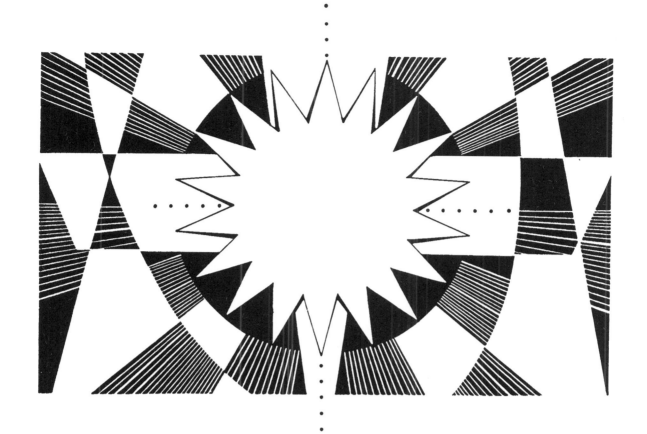

1

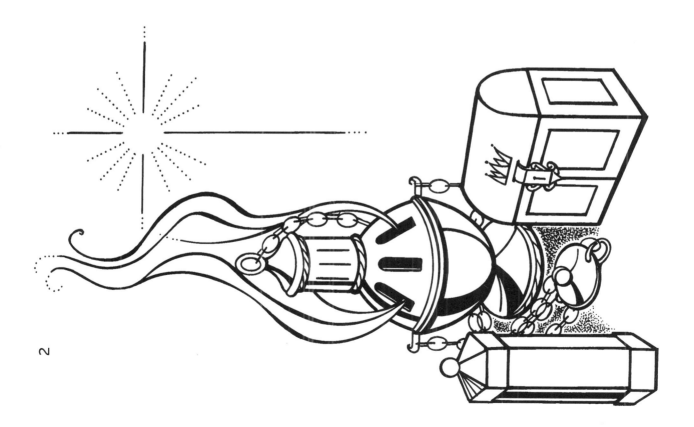

2

The Passion 1

The Passion 2

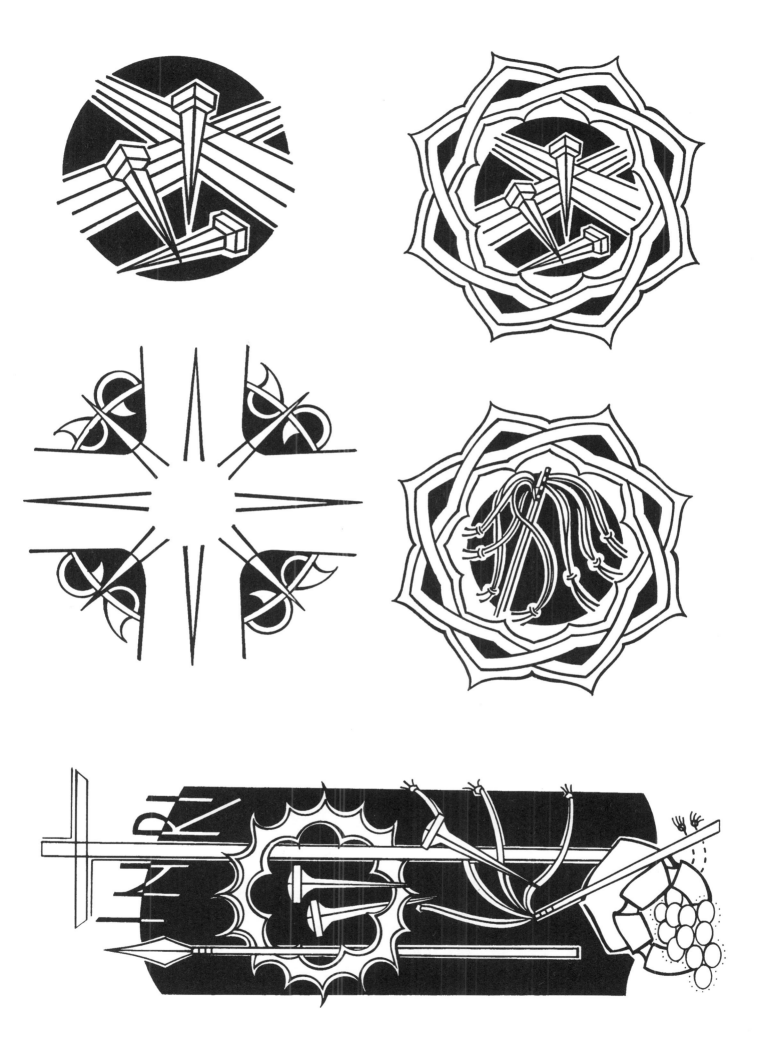

The Passion 3

Wood carvings of the Passion Flower
are frequently found in old churches.
The structure of the flower head suggests
the apostles gathered round Christ.
The crown of thorns, the five wounds and
the three nails complete the symbolism
of the Passion.

Symbols of the Eucharist 1

1 The cup that we bless is a
communion with the blood of Christ;
and the bread that we break is a
communion with the body of the Lord.
1 Corinthians 10:16

Do this as a memorial of me.
Luke 22:19

2 He feeds us with finest wheat.
Psalm 147:14

1

2

Symbols of the Eucharist 2

1   The miracle of the multiplication of the loaves and fishes.
    John 5:5-15

    A basket of five loaves and two fishes used as
    a symbol of the Eucharist from early times.

2   Fish with a basket of loaves.

    The fish was a secret symbol of Christianity
    in the persecuted Early Church. Symbol of Christ,
    it is shown here bearing the loaves of the Eucharist.

3   Unless a wheat grain falls into the earth and dies,
    it remains only a single grain;
    but if it dies
    it yields a rich harvest.
    John 12:24

1

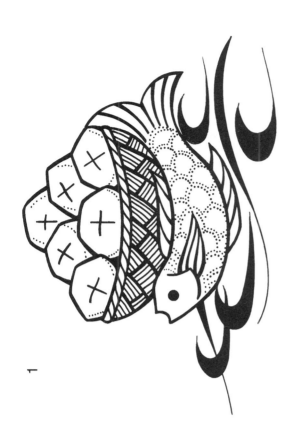

2

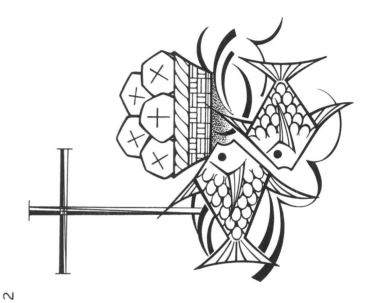

3

Easter Vigil

Paschal Candle

May the light of Christ, rising in glory,
dispel the darkness of our minds.

Easter

This day was made by the Lord,
we rejoice and are glad.

The Holy Spirit – Pentecost

The Sacraments 1

Baptism

Confirmation

Reconciliation

Eucharist

The Sacraments 1

Anointing of the sick

Holy Matrimony

Holy Orders

The Sacraments 2

Baptism: Symbols of the Rite

We are born to new life in Baptism.

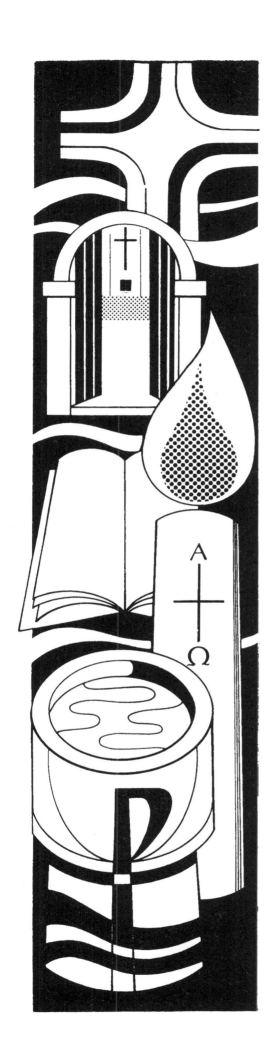

The Sacraments 2

Left   Eucharist

Right   Holy Matrimony

The Sacraments 2

Confirmation

The gifts of the Spirit are symbolised by the flames descending with the Dove. The 'fruits' of these gifts are suggested by the olive branch bearing olives.

Our Lady

Symbols of Our Lady

The lily, or a vase of lilies, traditionally
symbolises the sinlessness of Our Lady.

Hail, full of grace! The Lord is with you.
Luke 1:29

Left   Our Lady of Willesden

Right   Our Lady of Walsingham

The Cross 1

The Cross surrounded by a victor's laurel wreath preceded the more realistic portrayal of the Crucifixion after Constantine proclaimed the Peace of the Church in the fourth century.

Sometimes the Cross was decorated with jewels and semi-precious stones and, as in the first drawing opposite, the Christian symbolism of New Life is shown by shoots springing from each side of the Cross.

The Cross 2

An adaptation of a Middle Eastern pectoral cross from the sixth or seventh century. Stylised palms or palmettes in the arms of the cross symbolise Christ's victory over death.

The Cross 3

Tri-linear sixth-century designs on choir screens in the Church of Santa Sabina, Rome.

This form of ornamentation existed in the East and West, and was adopted in Rome where it flourished from the eighth to the twelfth century. It is assumed that the triad ornament symbolises the Holy Trinity, while the Cross is frequently found encircled with a wreath, and flanked by palms symbolising the Triumph of the Cross. Stylised vines and doves are similarly treated in connection with the Eucharist, and with Christ's words at the Last Supper: 'I am the vine and you are branches'.

1   The eagle representing Christ is at the centre of a cross formed by a triad braid. This braid is at the same time a vine. Christian souls in the form of small birds are feeding from the fruit.

2   A cross with triad or tri-linear interlacings with rosettes, open and closed, representing the sun and moon in the upper angles of the cross and stylised palms below.

2

1

Saints

All Saints

In every word and deed they spoke of Christ
and in their life gave glory to his name;
their love was unconsumed, a burning bush
of which the Holy Spirit was the flame.
Stanbrook Abbey Hymnal

God is the glory and joy of all his saints.

Symbols of Saints

1   The burning bush

2   Crown of glory and palm of martyrdom

3   A wheatsheaf symbolising the good wheat – the saints

1

2

3

St Columba

St Columba, whose name means dove, was responsible for the founding of Irish monasticism, and the spread of Christian learning. The boat, or coracle, symbolises his many sea journeys, and in particular the voyage to Iona where he founded a monastery. The book represents his enthusiasm for the production of Celtic illuminated manuscripts, and the crozier recalls his leadership and authority as an abbot.

St Michael

St Peter

St Agnes

The drawing is adapted from a seventh-century mosaic in the Basilica of St Agnes, Rome. She is dressed as a Byzantine princess, and the embroidered phoenix on her robe symbolises immortality. The sword of martyrdom lies at her feet.

St George

Celtic Design 1

Celtic ornamental foliage was rarely found until the Christian era. For example, the Tree of Life showing birds feeding among leafy scrolls is now intended to show the link between Christ and the Christian soul. 'I am the vine and you are the branches' *(John 15:5)*.

Used in a religious sense the continuous line formation in knots, interlacings and loops, reflects the Eternity of God. Three dots or circles, and the triquetra, showing three intersecting arcs, lead us to think of the Trinity.

Some of these elements have been used in the 'O' Antiphons and other designs in this book.

Celtic Design 2

Celtic Design 3

Symbolism of the Vine

Christ is the true vine and we are the branches.
Only through union with him are we able to share
in the mystery of the Eucharist.

Symbols from the Old Testament

1 The rainbow – the sign of God's covenant with the earth after the flood. (See Genesis 9:12-16.)

2 Let the heavens rejoice and earth be glad!
   Let the sea thunder, and all it holds!
   Psalm 96:11

3 Two deer drinking from the waters of salvation flowing from the foot of the cross.

   As a hart longs for running streams,
   so my soul longs for you, O God.
   Psalm 42:1

The Parables 1

The kingdom of heaven is like a dragnet cast into the sea.
It brings in a haul of all kinds.
Matthew 13:47

The Parables 2

1   The kingdom of heaven is like treasure
    hidden in a field which someone has found.
    Matthew 13:44

2   The kingdom of heaven is like a mustard
    seed which a man took and sowed in his field.
    Matthew 13:31

1

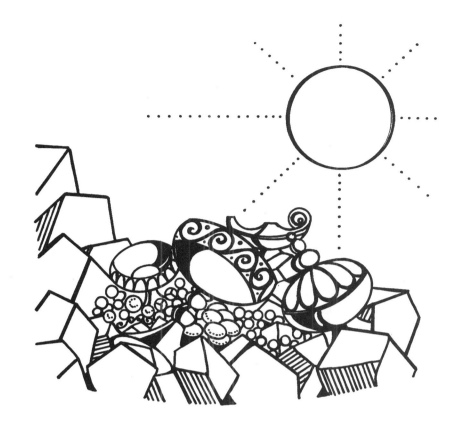

2

The Parables 3

1   The kingdom of heaven is like ten bridesmaids who
    took their lamps and went to meet the bridegroom.
    Matthew 25:1

2   The kingdom of heaven is like a lamp on a lampstand
    'for nothing is secret except to be brought to light'.
    Mark 4:21-22

3   The kingdom of heaven is like the good seed
    and the darnel among the wheat.
    Matthew 13:24-26

Words 1

STAY AWAKE

PRAY

LISTEN WATCH

WATCH LISTEN

PRAY

Words 2

Christmas
Greetings

✠Peace

O LORD
hear
my prayer

✠

Alleluia